My
Sweet
DESSERTS

Are you ready to cook
delicious Desserts?

Index

1 ....
2 ....
3 ....
4 ....
5 ....
6 ....
7 ....
8 ....
9 ....
10 ....
11 ....
12 ....
13 ....
14 ....
15 ....
16 ....
17 ....
18 ....
19 ....
20 ....
21 ....
22 ....
23 ....
24 ....
25 ....

Index

Index

Recipe Name

Prep. Time .... Cook Time ....

Difficulty .... Serves ....

⤳ Ingredients ⤘

....

....

....

....

⤳ Preparation ⤘

....

....

....

....

....

....

....

....

⤳ Notes ⤘

....

....

....

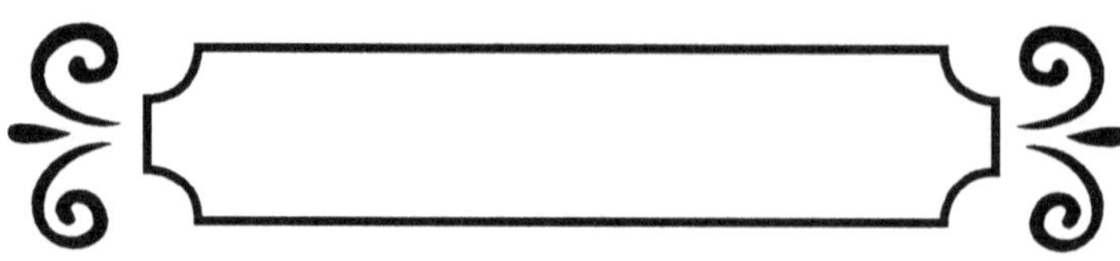

Recipe Name

Prep. Time .... **Cook Time** ....
Difficulty .... **Serves** ....

❧ Ingredients ❧

....
....
....
....

❧ Preparation ❧

....
....
....
....
....
....
....
....

❧ Notes ❧

....
....
....

Recipe Name

Prep. Time .... **Cook Time** ....
Difficulty .... **Serves** ....

❧ Ingredients ❧

....
....
....
....

❧ Preparation ❧

....
....
....
....
....
....
....
....

❧ Notes ❧

....
....
....

Recipe Name

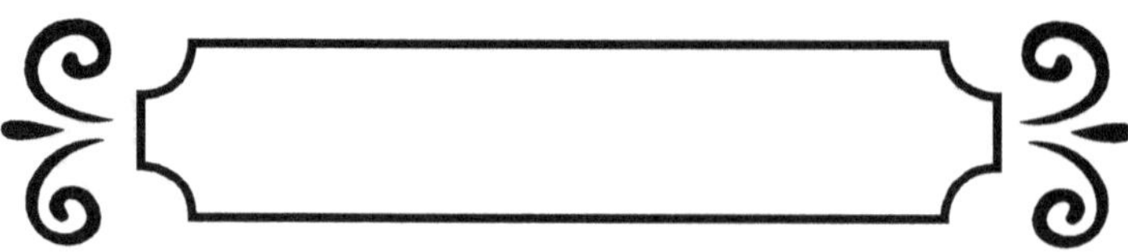

Prep. Time .... Cook Time ....

Difficulty .... Serves ....

❧ Ingredients ❧

❧ Preparation ❧

❧ Notes ❧

Recipe Name

Prep. Time .... Cook Time ....

Difficulty .... Serves ....

Ingredients

....

....

....

....

Preparation

....

....

....

....

....

....

....

....

Notes

....

....

....

Recipe Name

Prep. Time .... **Cook Time** ....
Difficulty .... **Serves** ....

❧ Ingredients ☙

....
....
....
....

❧ Preparation ☙

....
....
....
....
....
....
....
....

❧ Notes ☙

....
....
....

Recipe Name

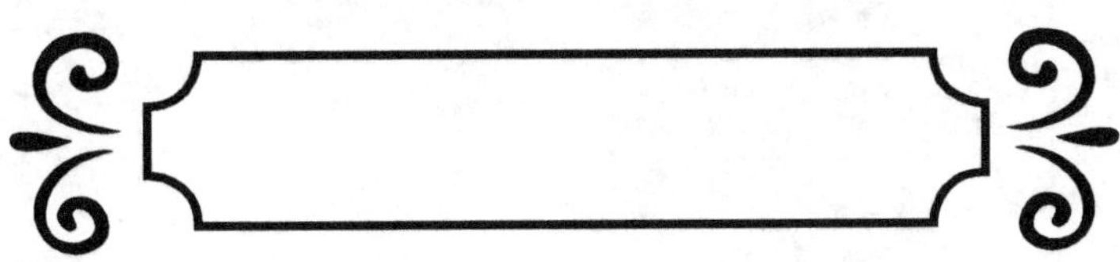

Prep. Time .... **Cook Time** ....

Difficulty .... **Serves** ....

Ingredients

....
....
....
....

Preparation

....
....
....
....
....
....
....
....

Notes

....
....
....

Recipe Name

Prep. Time .... Cook Time ....

Difficulty .... Serves ....

❧ Ingredients ☙

❧ Preparation ☙

❧ Notes ☙

Recipe Name

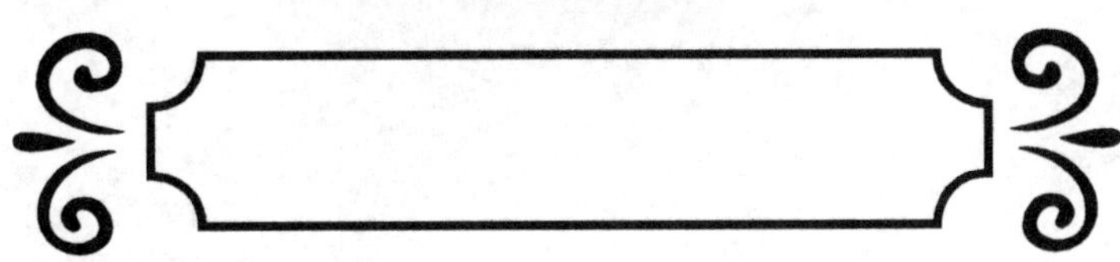

Prep. Time .... Cook Time ....

Difficulty .... Serves ....

❧ Ingredients ☙

....
....
....
....

❧ Preparation ☙

....
....
....
....
....
....
....
....

❧ Notes ☙

....
....
....

Recipe Name

Prep. Time .... Cook Time ....

Difficulty .... Serves ....

❧ Ingredients ☙

....

....

....

....

❧ Preparation ☙

....

....

....

....

....

....

....

....

❧ Notes ☙

....

....

....

Recipe Name

Prep. Time .... Cook Time ....
Difficulty .... Serves ....

Ingredients

....
....
....
....

Preparation

....
....
....
....
....
....
....
....

Notes

....
....
....

Recipe Name

Prep. Time .... Cook Time ....

Difficulty .... Serves ....

❧ Ingredients ❧

❧ Preparation ❧

❧ Notes ❧

Recipe Name

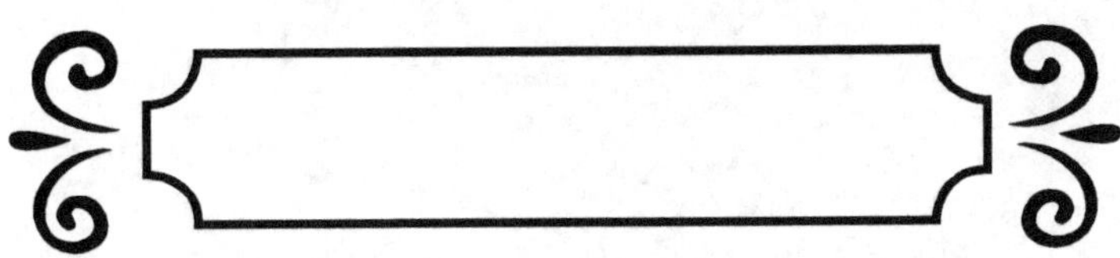

Prep. Time .... Cook Time ....
Difficulty .... Serves ....

❧ Ingredients ❧

....
....
....
....

❧ Preparation ❧

....
....
....
....
....
....
....
....

❧ Notes ❧

....
....
....

Recipe Name

Prep. Time .... Cook Time ....

Difficulty .... Serves ....

❧ Ingredients ☙

❧ Preparation ☙

❧ Notes ☙

Recipe Name

Prep. Time .... **Cook Time** ....

Difficulty .... **Serves** ....

❧ Ingredients ☙

....
....
....
....

❧ Preparation ☙

....
....
....
....
....
....
....
....

❧ Notes ☙

....
....
....

Recipe Name

Prep. Time .... **Cook Time** ....

Difficulty .... **Serves** ....

⇘ Ingredients ⇙

....

....

....

....

⇘ Preparation ⇙

....

....

....

....

....

....

....

....

⇘ Notes ⇙

....

....

....

Recipe Name

Prep. Time .... **Cook Time** ....
Difficulty .... **Serves** ....

⇘ Ingredients ⇙

....
....
....
....

⇘ Preparation ⇙

....
....
....
....
....
....
....
....

⇘ Notes ⇙

....
....
....

Recipe Name

Prep. Time .... Cook Time ....

Difficulty .... Serves ....

❧ Ingredients ❧

....

....

....

....

❧ Preparation ❧

....

....

....

....

....

....

....

....

❧ Notes ❧

....

....

....

Recipe Name

Prep. Time .... Cook Time ....
Difficulty .... Serves ....

❧ Ingredients ❧

....
....
....
....

❧ Preparation ❧

....
....
....
....
....
....
....
....

❧ Notes ❧

....
....
....

Recipe Name

Prep. Time .... Cook Time ....
Difficulty .... Serves ....

❧ Ingredients ☙

❧ Preparation ☙

❧ Notes ☙

Recipe Name

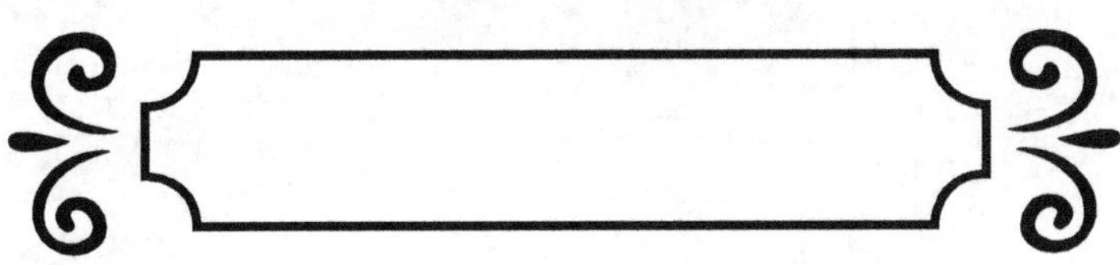

Prep. Time .... Cook Time ....

Difficulty .... Serves ....

Ingredients

Preparation

Notes

Recipe Name

Prep. Time .... Cook Time ....

Difficulty .... Serves ....

❧ Ingredients ☙

❧ Preparation ☙

❧ Notes ☙

Recipe Name

Prep. Time .... Cook Time ....

Difficulty .... Serves ....

❧ Ingredients ❧

....

....

....

....

❧ Preparation ❧

....

....

....

....

....

....

....

....

❧ Notes ❧

....

....

....

Recipe Name

Prep. Time .... Cook Time ....

Difficulty .... Serves ....

❧ Ingredients ❧

❧ Preparation ❧

❧ Notes ❧

Recipe Name

Prep. Time .... Cook Time ....
Difficulty .... Serves ....

Ingredients

Preparation

Notes

Recipe Name

Prep. Time .... Cook Time ....

Difficulty .... Serves ....

Ingredients

....

....

....

....

Preparation

....

....

....

....

....

....

....

....

Notes

....

....

....

Recipe Name

Prep. Time .... Cook Time ....

Difficulty .... Serves ....

⤳ Ingredients ⤲

....

....

....

....

⤳ Preparation ⤲

....

....

....

....

....

....

....

....

⤳ Notes ⤲

....

....

....

Recipe Name

Prep. Time .... Cook Time ....

Difficulty .... Serves ....

❧ Ingredients ☙

....

....

....

....

❧ Preparation ☙

....

....

....

....

....

....

....

....

❧ Notes ☙

....

....

....

Recipe Name

Prep. Time .... **Cook Time** ....
Difficulty .... **Serves** ....

❧ Ingredients ☙

....
....
....
....

❧ Preparation ☙

....
....
....
....
....
....
....
....

❧ Notes ☙

....
....
....

Recipe Name

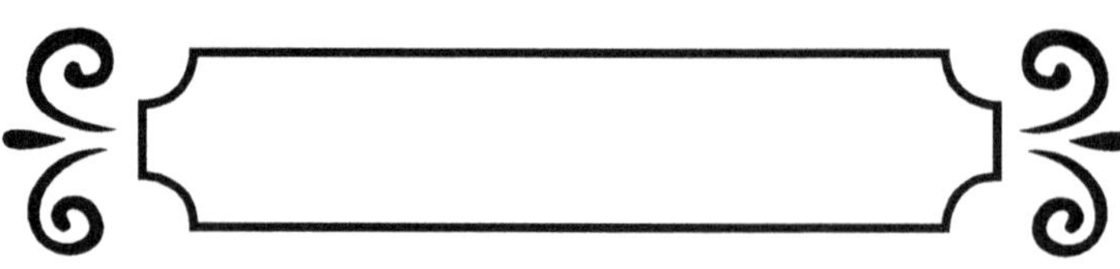

Prep. Time .... Cook Time ....

Difficulty .... Serves ....

❧ Ingredients ❧

❧ Preparation ❧

❧ Notes ❧

Recipe Name

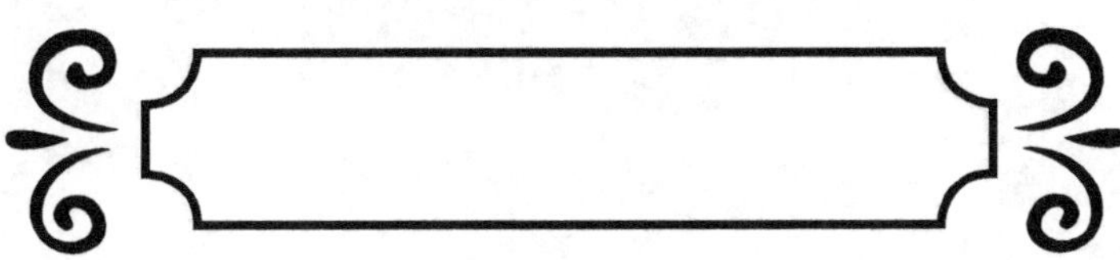

Prep. Time .... **Cook Time** ....

Difficulty .... **Serves** ....

❧ Ingredients ❧

....

....

....

....

❧ Preparation ❧

....

....

....

....

....

....

....

....

❧ Notes ❧

....

....

....

Recipe Name

Prep. Time .... Cook Time ....

Difficulty .... Serves ....

❧ Ingredients ❧

❧ Preparation ❧

❧ Notes ❧

Recipe Name

Prep. Time .... Cook Time ....

Difficulty .... Serves ....

❧ Ingredients ☙

....

....

....

....

❧ Preparation ☙

....

....

....

....

....

....

....

....

❧ Notes ☙

....

....

....

Recipe Name

Prep. Time .... Cook Time ....

Difficulty .... Serves ....

≫ Ingredients ≪

≫ Preparation ≪

≫ Notes ≪

Recipe Name

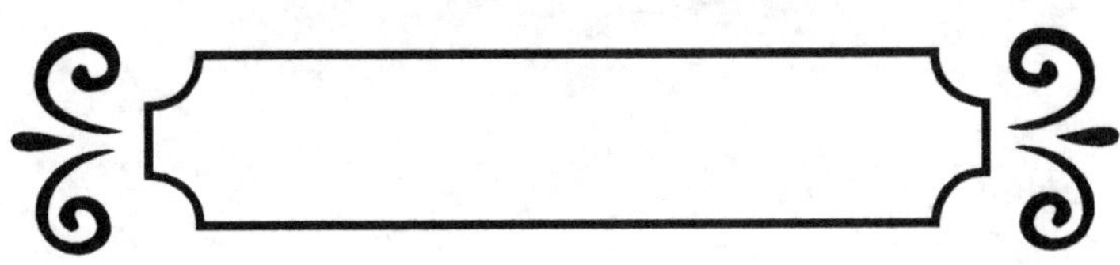

Prep. Time .... **Cook Time** ....

Difficulty .... **Serves** ....

❧ Ingredients ☙

....
....
....
....

❧ Preparation ☙

....
....
....
....
....
....
....
....

❧ Notes ☙

....
....
....

Recipe Name

Prep. Time .... **Cook Time** ....

Difficulty .... **Serves** ....

❧ Ingredients ❧

❧ Preparation ❧

❧ Notes ❧

Recipe Name

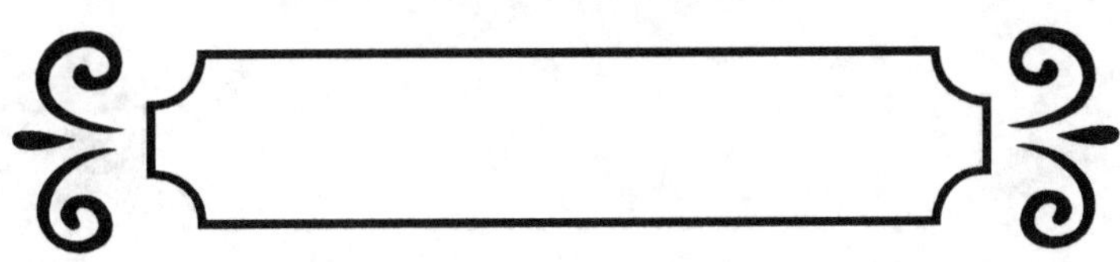

Prep. Time .... Cook Time ....
Difficulty .... Serves ....

❧ Ingredients ☙

....
....
....
....

❧ Preparation ☙

....
....
....
....
....
....
....
....

❧ Notes ☙

....
....
....

Recipe Name

Prep. Time .... Cook Time ....

Difficulty .... Serves ....

❧ Ingredients ❧

....

....

....

....

❧ Preparation ❧

....

....

....

....

....

....

....

....

❧ Notes ❧

....

....

....

Recipe Name

Prep. Time .... **Cook Time** ....

Difficulty .... **Serves** ....

❧ Ingredients ❧

....

....

....

....

❧ Preparation ❧

....

....

....

....

....

....

....

....

❧ Notes ❧

....

....

....

Recipe Name

Prep. Time .... **Cook Time** ....

Difficulty .... **Serves** ....

❧ Ingredients ☙

....

....

....

....

❧ Preparation ☙

....

....

....

....

....

....

....

....

❧ Notes ☙

....

....

....

Recipe Name

Prep. Time .... Cook Time ....
Difficulty .... Serves ....

❧ Ingredients ☙

....
....
....
....

❧ Preparation ☙

....
....
....
....
....
....
....
....

❧ Notes ☙

....
....
....

Recipe Name

Prep. Time .... Cook Time ....
Difficulty .... Serves ....

Ingredients

Preparation

Notes

Recipe Name

Prep. Time .... Cook Time ....

Difficulty .... Serves ....

❧ Ingredients ❦

....

....

....

....

❧ Preparation ❦

....

....

....

....

....

....

....

....

❧ Notes ❦

....

....

....

Recipe Name

Prep. Time .... Cook Time ....

Difficulty .... Serves ....

❧ Ingredients ☙

....

....

....

....

❧ Preparation ☙

....

....

....

....

....

....

....

....

❧ Notes ☙

....

....

....

Recipe Name

Prep. Time .... **Cook Time** ....

Difficulty .... **Serves** ....

Ingredients

Preparation

Notes

Recipe Name

Prep. Time .... Cook Time ....

Difficulty .... Serves ....

❧ Ingredients ❧

❧ Preparation ❧

❧ Notes ❧

Recipe Name

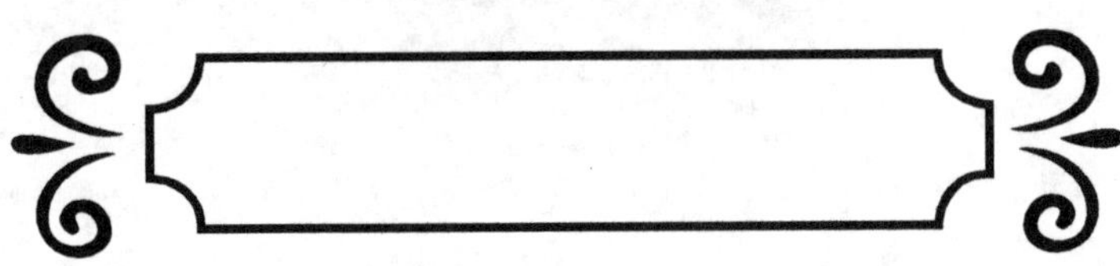

Prep. Time .... Cook Time ....

Difficulty .... Serves ....

❧ Ingredients ❧

....

....

....

....

❧ Preparation ❧

....

....

....

....

....

....

....

....

❧ Notes ❧

....

....

....

Recipe Name

Prep. Time .... Cook Time ....

Difficulty .... Serves ....

❧ Ingredients ☙

....

....

....

....

❧ Preparation ☙

....

....

....

....

....

....

....

....

❧ Notes ☙

....

....

....

Recipe Name

Prep. Time .... Cook Time ....

Difficulty .... Serves ....

❧ Ingredients ☙

....

....

....

....

❧ Preparation ☙

....

....

....

....

....

....

....

....

❧ Notes ☙

....

....

....

Recipe Name

Prep. Time .... Cook Time ....

Difficulty .... Serves ....

❧ Ingredients ☙

❧ Preparation ☙

❧ Notes ☙

Recipe Name

Prep. Time .... Cook Time ....

Difficulty .... Serves ....

❧ Ingredients ☙

....

....

....

....

❧ Preparation ☙

....

....

....

....

....

....

....

....

❧ Notes ☙

....

....

....

Recipe Name

Prep. Time .... Cook Time ....

Difficulty .... Serves ....

⇘ Ingredients ⇙

....

....

....

....

⇘ Preparation ⇙

....

....

....

....

....

....

....

....

⇘ Notes ⇙

....

....

....

Recipe Name

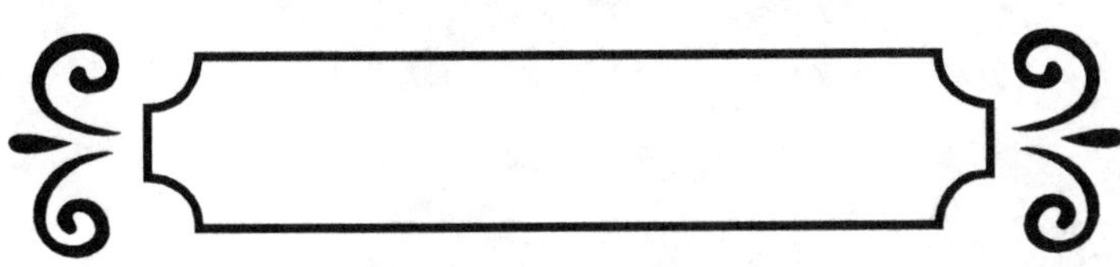

Prep. Time .... **Cook Time** ....

Difficulty .... **Serves** ....

⤷ Ingredients ⤶

....

....

....

....

⤷ Preparation ⤶

....

....

....

....

....

....

....

....

⤷ Notes ⤶

....

....

....

Recipe Name

Prep. Time .... Cook Time ....
Difficulty .... Serves ....

❧ Ingredients ❧

....
....
....
....

❧ Preparation ❧

....
....
....
....
....
....
....
....

❧ Notes ❧

....
....
....

Recipe Name

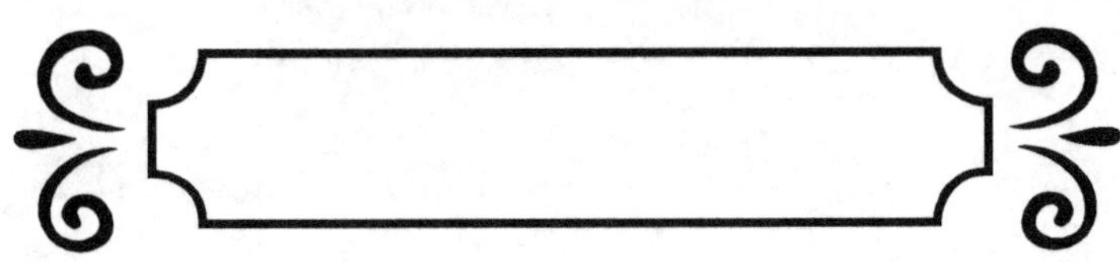

Prep. Time .... **Cook Time** ....
Difficulty .... **Serves** ....

Ingredients

....
....
....
....

Preparation

....
....
....
....
....
....
....
....

Notes

....
....
....

Recipe Name

Prep. Time .... **Cook Time** ....

Difficulty .... **Serves** ....

❧ Ingredients ❧

❧ Preparation ❧

❧ Notes ❧

Recipe Name

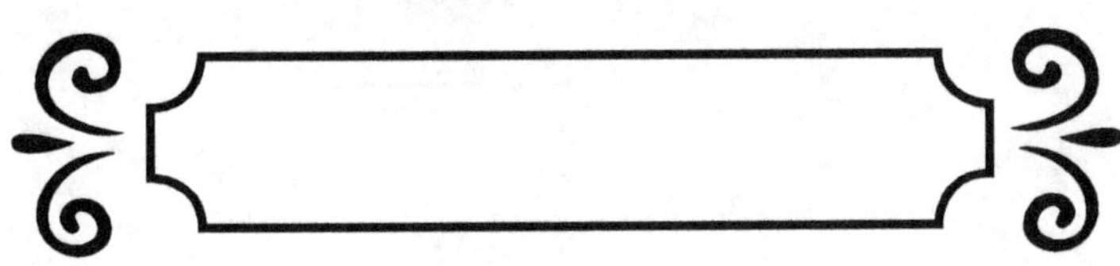

Prep. Time .... Cook Time ....
Difficulty .... Serves ....

⇘ Ingredients ⇙

....
....
....
....

⇘ Preparation ⇙

....
....
....
....
....
....
....
....

⇘ Notes ⇙

....
....
....

Recipe Name

Prep. Time .... Cook Time ....

Difficulty .... Serves ....

❧ Ingredients ☙

....

....

....

....

❧ Preparation ☙

....

....

....

....

....

....

....

....

❧ Notes ☙

....

....

....

Recipe Name

Prep. Time .... **Cook Time** ....
Difficulty .... **Serves** ....

≥ Ingredients ≤

....
....
....
....

≥ Preparation ≤

....
....
....
....
....
....
....
....

≥ Notes ≤

....
....
....

Recipe Name

Prep. Time .... Cook Time ....

Difficulty .... Serves ....

❧ Ingredients ❧

❧ Preparation ❧

❧ Notes ❧

Recipe Name

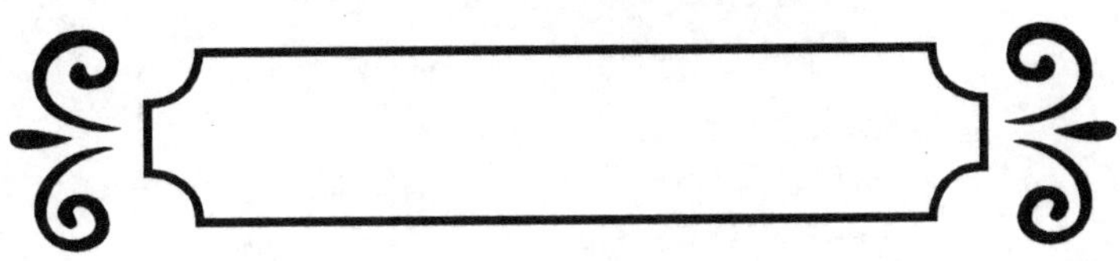

Prep. Time .... **Cook Time** ....

Difficulty .... **Serves** ....

❧ Ingredients ❧

....

....

....

....

❧ Preparation ❧

....

....

....

....

....

....

....

....

❧ Notes ❧

....

....

....

Prep. Time .... Cook Time ....

Difficulty .... Serves ....

❧ Ingredients ❧

....

....

....

....

❧ Preparation ❧

....

....

....

....

....

....

....

....

❧ Notes ❧

....

....

....

Recipe Name

Prep. Time .... **Cook Time** ....

Difficulty .... **Serves** ....

❧ Ingredients ❧

....
....
....
....

❧ Preparation ❧

....
....
....
....
....
....
....
....

❧ Notes ❧

....
....
....

Recipe Name

Prep. Time .... Cook Time ....

Difficulty .... Serves ....

❧ Ingredients ☙

❧ Preparation ☙

❧ Notes ☙

Recipe Name

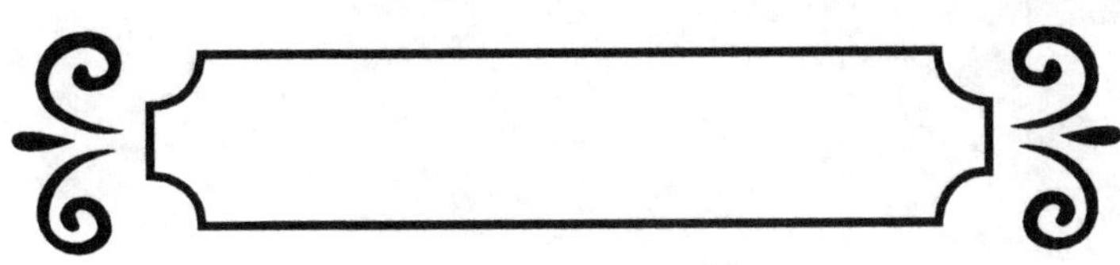

Prep. Time .... **Cook Time** ....

Difficulty .... **Serves** ....

❧ Ingredients ❧

....

....

....

....

❧ Preparation ❧

....

....

....

....

....

....

....

....

❧ Notes ❧

....

....

....

Recipe Name

Prep. Time .... Cook Time ....
Difficulty .... Serves ....

⇘ Ingredients ⇙

....
....
....
....

⇘ Preparation ⇙

....
....
....
....
....
....
....
....

⇘ Notes ⇙

....
....
....

Recipe Name

Prep. Time .... Cook Time ....
Difficulty .... Serves ....

❧ Ingredients ❧

❧ Preparation ❧

❧ Notes ❧

Recipe Name

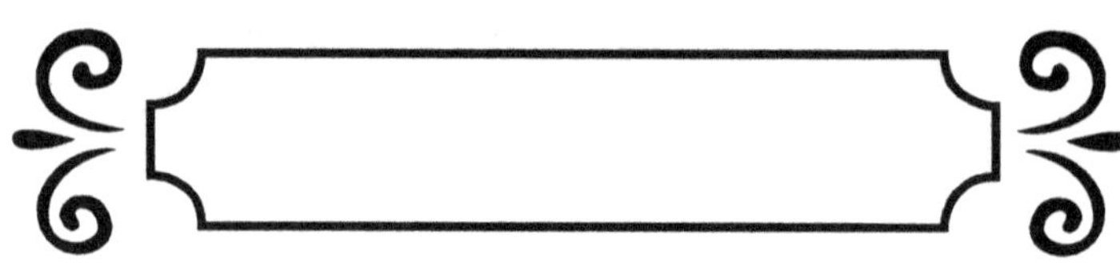

Prep. Time .... **Cook Time** ....

Difficulty .... **Serves** ....

⇘ Ingredients ⇙

⇘ Preparation ⇙

⇘ Notes ⇙

Recipe Name

Prep. Time .... Cook Time ....
Difficulty .... Serves ....

Ingredients

Preparation

Notes

Recipe Name

Prep. Time .... Cook Time ....
Difficulty .... Serves ....

✣ Ingredients ✣

....
....
....
....

✣ Preparation ✣

....
....
....
....
....
....
....
....

✣ Notes ✣

....
....
....

Recipe Name

Prep. Time .... Cook Time ....

Difficulty .... Serves ....

❧ Ingredients ☙

....

....

....

....

❧ Preparation ☙

....

....

....

....

....

....

....

....

❧ Notes ☙

....

....

....

Recipe Name

Prep. Time .... Cook Time ....

Difficulty .... Serves ....

᎒ Ingredients ᎒

᎒ Preparation ᎒

᎒ Notes ᎒

Recipe Name

Prep. Time .... **Cook Time** ....
Difficulty .... **Serves** ....

⇘ Ingredients ⇙

....
....
....
....

⇘ Preparation ⇙

....
....
....
....
....
....
....
....

⇘ Notes ⇙

....
....
....

Recipe Name

Prep. Time .... Cook Time ....
Difficulty .... Serves ....

❧ Ingredients ☙

....
....
....
....

❧ Preparation ☙

....
....
....
....
....
....
....
....

❧ Notes ☙

....
....
....

Recipe Name

Prep. Time .... **Cook Time** ....
Difficulty .... **Serves** ....

Ingredients

....
....
....
....

Preparation

....
....
....
....
....
....
....
....

Notes

....
....
....

Recipe Name

Prep. Time .... **Cook Time** ....

Difficulty .... **Serves** ....

❧ Ingredients ☙

....

....

....

....

❧ Preparation ☙

....

....

....

....

....

....

....

❧ Notes ☙

....

....

....

Recipe Name

Prep. Time .... Cook Time ....

Difficulty .... Serves ....

❧ Ingredients ❧

....

....

....

....

❧ Preparation ❧

....

....

....

....

....

....

....

....

❧ Notes ❧

....

....

....

Recipe Name

Prep. Time .... Cook Time ....
Difficulty .... Serves ....

❧ Ingredients ☙

❧ Preparation ☙

❧ Notes ☙

Recipe Name

Prep. Time .... **Cook Time** ....

Difficulty .... **Serves** ....

Ingredients

Preparation

Notes

Recipe Name

Prep. Time .... Cook Time ....
Difficulty .... Serves ....

❧ Ingredients ❧

❧ Preparation ❧

❧ Notes ❧

Recipe Name

Prep. Time .... **Cook Time** ....

Difficulty .... **Serves** ....

Ingredients

....

....

....

....

Preparation

....

....

....

....

....

....

....

....

Notes

....

....

....

Recipe Name

Prep. Time .... Cook Time ....
Difficulty .... Serves ....

❧ Ingredients ❧

❧ Preparation ❧

❧ Notes ❧

Recipe Name

Prep. Time .... **Cook Time** ....

Difficulty .... **Serves** ....

❧ Ingredients ❧

....

....

....

....

❧ Preparation ❧

....

....

....

....

....

....

....

....

❧ Notes ❧

....

....

....

Recipe Name

Prep. Time .... Cook Time ....

Difficulty .... Serves ....

⇾ Ingredients ⇽

....

....

....

....

⇾ Preparation ⇽

....

....

....

....

....

....

....

....

⇾ Notes ⇽

....

....

....

Recipe Name

Prep. Time .... Cook Time ....

Difficulty .... Serves ....

❧ Ingredients ☙

....
....
....
....

❧ Preparation ☙

....
....
....
....
....
....
....
....

❧ Notes ☙

....
....
....

Recipe Name

Prep. Time .... **Cook Time** ....
Difficulty .... **Serves** ....

Ingredients

Preparation

Notes

Recipe Name

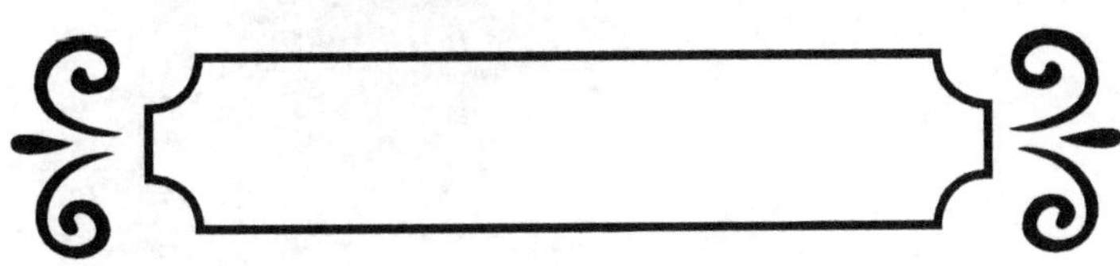

Prep. Time .... Cook Time ....

Difficulty .... Serves ....

Ingredients

....

....

....

....

Preparation

Notes

Recipe Name

Prep. Time .... Cook Time ....
Difficulty .... Serves ....

⇘ Ingredients ⇙

⇘ Preparation ⇙

⇘ Notes ⇙

Recipe Name

Prep. Time .... Cook Time ....
Difficulty .... Serves ....

Ingredients

....
....
....
....

Preparation

....
....
....
....
....
....
....
....

Notes

....
....
....

Recipe Name

Prep. Time .... Cook Time ....
Difficulty .... Serves ....

Ingredients

....
....
....
....

Preparation

....
....
....
....
....
....
....
....

Notes

....
....
....

Recipe Name

Prep. Time .... Cook Time ....
Difficulty .... Serves ....

❧ Ingredients ❧

....
....
....
....

❧ Preparation ❧

....
....
....
....
....
....
....
....

❧ Notes ❧

....
....
....

Recipe Name

Prep. Time .... **Cook Time** ....
Difficulty .... **Serves** ....

❧ Ingredients ☙

....
....
....
....

❧ Preparation ☙

....
....
....
....
....
....
....
....

❧ Notes ☙

....
....
....

Recipe Name

Prep. Time .... **Cook Time** ....

Difficulty .... **Serves** ....

❧ Ingredients ☙

....

....

....

....

❧ Preparation ☙

....

....

....

....

....

....

....

....

❧ Notes ☙

....

....

....

Recipe Name

Prep. Time .... **Cook Time** ....

Difficulty .... **Serves** ....

❧ Ingredients ☙

....

....

....

....

❧ Preparation ☙

....

....

....

....

....

....

....

....

❧ Notes ☙

....

....

....

Recipe Name

Prep. Time .... Cook Time ....
Difficulty .... Serves ....

≫ Ingredients ≪

....
....
....
....

≫ Preparation ≪

....
....
....
....
....
....
....
....

≫ Notes ≪

....
....
....

Recipe Name

Prep. Time .... **Cook Time** ....
Difficulty .... **Serves** ....

⟡ Ingredients ⟡

....

....

....

....

⟡ Preparation ⟡

....

....

....

....

....

....

....

....

⟡ Notes ⟡

....

....

....

Recipe Name

Prep. Time .... Cook Time ....
Difficulty .... Serves ....

❧ Ingredients ❧

....
....
....
....

❧ Preparation ❧

....
....
....
....
....
....
....
....

❧ Notes ❧

....
....
....

Recipe Name

Prep. Time .... **Cook Time** ....

Difficulty .... **Serves** ....

❧ Ingredients ☙

....
....
....
....

❧ Preparation ☙

....
....
....
....
....
....
....
....

❧ Notes ☙

....
....
....

Recipe Name

Prep. Time .... **Cook Time** ....
Difficulty .... **Serves** ....

❧ Ingredients ☙

....
....
....
....

❧ Preparation ☙

....
....
....
....
....
....
....
....

❧ Notes ☙

....
....
....

Recipe Name

Prep. Time .... **Cook Time** ....

Difficulty .... **Serves** ....

❧ Ingredients ☙

....

....

....

....

❧ Preparation ☙

....

....

....

....

....

....

....

....

❧ Notes ☙

....

....

....

CPSIA information can be obtained
at www.ICGtesting.com
Printed in the USA
LVHW080532141120
671499LV00007B/414